SOMEBODY BLEW UP AMERICA
& OTHER POEMS

BOOKS BY HOUSE OF NEHESI PUBLISHERS

The Essence of Reparations
Amiri Baraka

1963 - A Landmark Year in St. Martin
A Retrospective Look
Daniella Jeffry-Pilot

The House That Jack Built and Other Plays
Louie Laveist

Saint-Martin: Objectif statut - repères pour l'espoir
Edité par Consensus Populaire Saint-Martinois

Same Sea . . . Another Wave
Cynthia Wilson

St. Martin Massive!
A Snapshot of Popular Artists
House of Nehesi Publishers Special Edition

Words Need Love Too
Kamau Brathwaite

Coming, Coming Home - Conversations II
Western Education & The Caribbean Intellectual
George Lamming

Regreso, regreso al hogar - Conversaciones II
La educación occidental y el intelectual Caribeño
George Lamming

The Republic of St. Martin
Joseph H. Lake, Jr.

Songs & Images of St. Martin
Charles Borromeo Hodge

The Rainy Season
Drisana Deborah Jack

Brotherhood of The Spurs
(fiction, short stories)
Lasana M. Sekou

SOMEBODY BLEW UP AMERICA

& OTHER POEMS

AMIRI BARAKA

HOUSE OF NEHESI PUBLISHERS
P.O. Box 460
Philipsburg, St. Martin
Caribbean

WWW.HOUSEOFNEHESIPUBLISH.COM

Cover and graphics design by Lisa Hamilton
Cover art: "A Baraka" 2003, charcoal by Joe Dominique
Digital illustrations by Angelo Rombley

For Amina, for ever

CONTENTS

INTRODUCTION

Certain things seem fairly obvious when one comes to talk about Amiri Baraka. He is a poet, but more often than not, when we do hear about him, read about him or even hear from him, we hear little about his poetry. We hear a great deal about some lines, some words in his poems, and a marvelously complex legend of controversy that surrounds him, but very little of this is about poems, about the art of poetry, about the place of poetry in society. The problem with introducing Baraka is that he is simply one of those people who we can safely assume needs no introduction. Yet, therein lies the problem with Baraka.

This peculiar situation has characterized my encounter with Baraka again and again. Read Baraka's rationale and manifesto for the Black Arts Theater Movement and then read or view his brilliant play *Dutchman*, and you find a peculiar disconnect. Baraka does not do what he says he will do. Baraka, instead, creates a play that defies polemics, which is filled with ambiguities, complicated contradictions--a play that is as much an indictment of white racist society as it is of the collusion of Black middle class *naïveté*. There are no easy villains and victims in *Dutchman*. At least not in the way I read it. This is why it is a significant play. Yet, Baraka's declaration of aesthetic war seems to have been ignored in the writing of the play. Read Baraka's *Blues People* and you are left with a powerfully sophisticated reading of the history of blues aesthetic in African-American and American culture. There is no worn polemic there--nothing of the demon. Still, Baraka is not afraid of the demonized image of himself that people have.

Baraka will tease us, toy with us, play with us, undermine us. He is the guy who stands on the playground teasing someone. We watch him and we find what he is saying funny because we always felt the same way about the guy he is teasing. So we think, "Hey, this guy is cool, let me join him." Yet, the moment we open our mouths to start to throw insults, he turns on us. He changes the game. Or sometimes, he takes it further, as if he is trying to test us, now, and not the person he is teasing. He goes so far and we are left bedlamized in the middle--not sure where we stand. We stand there dumbfounded. We feel betrayed, and he is grinning. We walk away shaking our heads. This revolutionary figure does not offer us easy paths to the revolution.

Of course, all this may seem like pointless game playing--an artist engaged less in the issues but more in the impact of his treatment of the issues. I do not think that is a fair way to regard Baraka. It may be more accurate to suggest that Baraka does not simply accept anyone who says they are a revolutionary as a revolutionary. He wants the self-proclaimed revolutionary to be able to articulate the rationale of his or her beliefs. He is not looking for followers--he is looking for free thinkers. Baraka is engaged in an intellectual project--one that demands a clarity of understanding and a self-actualized sense of commitment that is rooted in understanding. If you say you are a revolutionary, he will test that claim. His political intentions are rooted in an unquestioning devotion to the celebration and defense of work that grows out of the Black aesthetic. He has always been articulate about Third World politics and the condition of the African-American in the USA. His grasp of the anger and despair in Black America is acutely expressed in much of his work. Indeed, it is the voicing of this anger that we often recall most about Baraka--it is this that has come to shape the way people react to him.

I have tried, with some difficulty, to follow the mess of views, counter-views surrounding Baraka and his now infamous poem, "Somebody Blew Up America," which is the title poem of this collection. I am left with one recourse: to turn to the poetry to see if I can find in the poem a truth that can help me to understand more of what his artistic legacy really is. It is hard to do this free of the clutter of views, of the pontifications, of the claims, of the legend, but at the end of the day, the poem is in a book that is full of words, and somehow we can arrive at some place of understanding the words by careful reading and thought.

I know this much, many people are upset with Baraka. He has angered those who think that he has somehow besmirched the pure horror and clear-eyed moral repugnancy of the attack of the World Trade Center in 2001 by suggesting, somehow, that someone, other than the terrorists, knew about the attack and may have in fact taken action to ensure that at least some of the people who worked at the center be warned to stay home before the attack:

> Who knew the World Trade center was gonna get
> bombed
>
> who told 4000 Israeli workers at the Twin Towers
> to stay home that day
>
> why did Sharon stay away ?

It would be quibbling to say that it is merely a question. It is a little stronger than that--it is an implication, and given the weight of the issue, it is, indeed, a contention. And this upsets many because it argues that someone other than the terrorists may have colluded in the act. Left like this, the poem is easily an incendiary piece. After all, it implicates Israel in the matter. The question I want to pose here is, is this enough to stop us from reading the rest of Baraka's poem and the rest of his book? Is this a fitting introduction to the man's work and does it effectively encapsulate the entirety of the work? I am introducing you to Baraka's book, and in so doing, I am asking you to read on. I ask you to do so understanding that what you read may confirm everything you have felt before hand, thus providing you with greater rationale for your view; or the work may somehow complicate what you think you know and offer other ways of seeing what Baraka is trying to say. I offer this introduction in many ways as one who believes that the text should be granted a certain respect--even a certain autonomy outside of the statements made by the author of that text. There is a deep ethical problem with completely expunging the author from any discussion of the text, but I do like to begin with the text.

Still, I have to be aware that it is a vain concept to think that the text is everything. It is vain, even if it remains a safe haven for the intellectual. The truth, though, is more complex. Baraka knows that. His entire agenda is predicated on the notion that one must always read the text in the context of society. Baraka is a public poet. That has been his positioning for years, and he has come to perfect that art. He is also an agitator. He has created an aesthetic that is intent on the public poem, the public art. The lyrical may crawl into his work now and then, but such moments seem like indulgences--moments of fancy forgetfulness. The rest is public and the aesthetic that comes through is a carefully cultivated one. It is not easily traced to the places to which we think it ought to be traced. After all, some have called Baraka a griot--a warrior/ priest/ politician/ poet in the West African tradition. It is an attractive label, but for Baraka it does not always work. The griot is rarely radical. The griot is rooted in tradition. The griot's function has always been to carry the stories of the tribe, to sing praises to the nation's leaders, to be present at weddings, funerals and other social gatherings with songs of celebration. The traditional griot is a priest, a musician and a spokesperson for the community. The griot's palette is not always political; it is as varied as society is varied. But the griot understands that his or her art is destined for the public and is given in service of the public--not simply to teach, but to speak for, speak about and celebrate the community. There are elements of the griot in Baraka, but he departs from the griot in some important ways. Baraka is rarely comfortable with the role of an "on-demand" poet whose words must conform to some predetermined aesthetic. He is positioned as a voice challenging the status-quo--a position not normally associated with the traditional griot. And where the griot functions in a society that values the poet, Baraka lives in a world in which the poet is seen as increasingly irrelevant. His work is engaged with the task of trying to challenge that notion. His is, then, an inherently antagonistic voice. Ironically, the naming of Baraka as Poet Laureate is akin to naming him a griot for the people and tribe of the state of New Jersey. He has clearly been at work at testing the limits of that title.

To read Baraka one should grasp something of his history, his journey as a writer, which has taken him toward a conception of the Blues as a functional aesthetic that speaks to the African-American experience. He has constantly been involved with the task of shaping an aesthetic whether it is for Black theater or for Black writing in general. As with all theorists who are artists as well, Baraka builds theoretical frameworks that he must challenge and break as an artist. This tension is critical if we are to find the space and the energy to tackle his poetry. The poems in this new collection, *Somebody Blew Up America & Other Poems*, reflect a poet who is busy recognizing the function of legacy and the role that he plays as a keeper of a community's history and sense of self. There is an introspection here that many might not expect of Baraka. There is also something of despair, a deep concern that much that is wrong in the world is either being ignored or missed by those who should be most concerned about it. As a result, the poems begin with alarm:

When the Beast emerged from the western sea
as a fictitious ghost who was an actual ghost

to the niggers He carried in his pouch of filth
his Moby Dick ship called Jesus to trick Jesse
and the one legged man who was the Beast
caught the big red Satan and threw him in a cage
disguised in a zoot suit, full of rage, he had fell
from the sky, thought he was an angel, looking
for an angle, a big red Satan, a black devil,
the money lenders created, when his father
was exiled headless in Patmos, looking at sky vision
and the horses ran by stinking up the sky

("Beginnings: Malcolm")

The explosion of images is intentionally wide ranging. Baraka understands that he writes out of and back to a western mythos, seeking, in the process, to challenge it and in some ways undermine it. But he also expects us to know that the reference to Patmos is an allusion to the book of *Revelation*, and that his poem is seeking to recast the ideas of apocalypse through the eyes of contemporary symbology. So Jesse may well be Jesse Jackson, even though there is a sense in which Jesus could be read as one who has effectively tricked the Jesse of the bible, from whose seed Jesus is said to have emerged (Jesse being the father of David). The allusion to Herman Melville's *Moby Dick* is not a new one for Baraka who has found ways to exploit the sexual and the literary implications of celebrating a figure like Melville whose work that deals with race is as much a part of the disturbing aesthetic of writing about race in America as anything written by William Faulkner.

I tease out this handful of allusions not to explain Baraka, but to point out that reading him requires a willingness to travel with him along the jazz inflected improvisations of rhythm and "sampling" that characterizes much of his poetic style. Yet, in "Beginnings: Malcolm" we also understand that Baraka offers a lyrical vulnerability in this sequence of poems as he begins to position himself as prophet and poet.

At the end of the poem there is the manner in which he connects himself with the tragic figure of Malcolm X.

> Was Black Betty there, Betty, beautiful, looking into
> the prophet's eyes
> following him inside blackness with the tales of her
> fire with the fiery tail
> with the kiss divine, like the poet's Amina, sitting there
> staring at the once Satanic
> issue, like joy from a hidden fissure in the earth,
> oh woman of the beginning, oh wife
> of the prophet, O, Lover!

Here lament and a lyric manner combine in a passage that reveals something of how Amiri Baraka understands himself --a figure who finds solace in love and affection even as he faces what he sees as a hostile world.

The Baraka we meet in *Somebody Blew Up America & Other Poems* is reminding us constantly that he is studying his people and trying to speak what they are experiencing. Images of seeing, of observing, of being something of a watchman in his community permeate these works. In the poem "In Town" he writes: "I can see something in the way of ourselves/That's why I say the things I do. You know it/But it's something else to you..." Later the language is repeated, reminding us that the world he is seeking to voice is one in which people can see, but are incapable of describing. There is a dumbness that has been foisted on people--Baraka wants to break that silence:

> You seen what I see too. A smile that ain't a smile but
>   teeth flying against our necks
> You see something too, but can't call its name.
>
> Aint it too bad, yall said. Aint it too bad.
> Such a nice boy. Always kind to his mother. Always
>   say good morning to everybody, on his way to
>   work. But that last time before he got locked up
>   and hurt
> Real bad I seen him walking toward his house and he

> wasn't smiling and he didn't
> even say Hello. But I knew he'd seen
> something. Something in the way of things.
> And it worked on him, like it do and will. ...

The poem becomes a sensitively rendered piece about the powerlessness of those who must contend with racism in contemporary society. Tellingly, Baraka is struck by the tyranny of silence that has somehow replaced the effort at outspoken expression of anger at racism. In a world in which it has become increasingly difficult for someone to speak of racism for fear of being called oversensitive and having a chip on the shoulder, Baraka's poem becomes a complex response. Here the "victim" has virtually forgotten his/her own pain:

> ... There is in that face, and remember,
> now, remember all them other faces
> And all the many places you seen him or the sister
> with his child wandering up the
> street. Remember what you seen in your own mirror,
> and didn' for a second
> recognize the face, your own face, straining to get out
> from behind the glass.

This business of calling a thing by its name has been a career for Baraka. It is clearly a path filled with potential treacheries and a path that he celebrates in the individuals that he regards as truth-sayers. In "Beginnings: Malcolm" he continues to reprise the lament for the dead--the lament for the heroic dead. He returns to the idea of the conspiracies that shaped Malcolm X's assassination, and he locates the narrative in the language of the Apocalypse--the diabolic forces that destroyed Malcolm X named as the Beast--an association that echoes the language of RasTafarianism that has, for decades referred to all instruments of government authority (including policemen and soldiers) as "beasts." For Baraka, the destruction of Malcolm X has not remained limited to him, but has been extended toward his family, and in that final moment in the poem, he enters his signature in the manner of a rap artist or a deejay. It is as close as Baraka will come to a poem of lyrical confession in a protest poem:

> But The Beast Had Tracked
>   Their children
>   Tracked them with
>   toilet breath
>   of lies
>
> O, Save Quibilah! we cried
>   Amina and I
>   sent Farrakhan a
>   plea. Just as we sd
>   to Betty
>
>   Struggle is constant
>   But we must
>   Unite
>   Follow the Fire
>   the Light!

Still there is in Baraka a certitude about the world that is for him easily and sharply drawn into camps of what is good and what is evil. His clarity is enviable, even if one is left with a sense of doubt. For Baraka, there is no room for nuance. He defines. In the poem "Understanding Readiness" something of a manifesto for the struggle is laid out. The poem is a celebration of Kwame Toure, and yet it reminds us of something that is unsaid--something that Baraka is clearly struggling with. The lament for the dead leaves him acutely aware of the absence of leaders that may have had the authority and status of a Kwame Toure. It is what leads Baraka to ask the question in "Understanding Readiness": "Who is it that will take this brother's place?" This question, like the many asked in the poem, are powerful ones--questions that remind us of the crisis of leadership in the Black community. The problem, though, lies in the answers:

> All of those who understand what his life was,
> what he wanted, what he did, and who, in the

end, he looked to as comrades in struggle,
whatever their names or philosophies
or ideologies or uniforms, or preparation.
All who want democracy and freedom.

We ask, is this enough? Baraka will not help us to answer
the question and we suddenly become aware that what he is
doing here is to celebrate Toure--as a warrior, as a figure that
is larger than life. This is a praise song in the classical West
African tradition. It is not a polemic--not a statement of polit-
ical creed. For that, Baraka must write a paper or make a
speech. For that, Baraka must walk away from those familiar
phrases that we have grown to expect in the rhetoric of praise
and struggle--in the public sphere of the political poem--
phrases that appear all over the poem ("help unite and liber-
ate oppressed people," "will struggle and be free").

The modes and moods in the collection are varied and
allow us to recognize in Baraka a layering of ideas and
themes that constantly turn on themselves. At times, one has
the feeling that he is writing back to himself--arguing with the
persona he has formed and finding a chance to correct him-
self, rewrite himself and recreate himself. At times, also, he
understands how he is seen by others and intentionally un-
dermines those ideas. Yet he also recognizes the power of
ironically confronting people with the images they have--he
confronts them by appropriating the images that they have of
him, and in a moment of irony akin to the trickster manner of
many a hip-hop artist, he assumes the mask of dangerous
man--he tosses it in the face of those who he knows will fear
it. In "Jungle Jim Flunks His Screen Test" Baraka cleverly plays
with the metaphor of a children's game and plays the dou-
bles with his readers. It is a cussing poem about ugliness. It
is funny, but only if you are willing to become a part of an
attack that might implicate you in something vitriolic. Baraka
is smart enough not to identify the object of his attack, be-

cause the poem is really not about the person who is ugly. The poem is about the similes about ugliness. The poem is indeed a catalogue of the things that Baraka regards as ugly. The catalogue is a telling one--it appears to be an equal opportunities catalogue:

You uglier than Papa Doc, Hitler and Mobutu
You uglier than Mussolini Franco
and the Swedish Angel
Is yr twin. You uglier than zombie vomit.
Uglier than zoo dirt. You the ugliest thing in the
human family
And that ID you got sayin' you human is ugly
You ugly as devil doo doo, white supremacy and you
Is identical. You ugly as the brain emptiness of a
cracker lynch mob.
You ugly as Falwell dressed as Cab Calloway. You
uglier than white people.

Yet we realize that there is in Amiri Baraka a narrative of race that quite easily positions whiteness as dangerously diabolic. Baraka's poetics in this regard were certainly more pronounced in his earlier days, but the vestiges of that project--that of trying to foreground the western iconography of positioning Blackness as evil and whiteness as good by reversing it--emerge in much of his new work. Today, ironically, such language seems more incendiary, dangerous and the Manichaean politics that shape this kind of imagery is exactly the kind of assured ethical absolutism that can sometimes seem a thing of the past. Yet Baraka must know that in many ways this discourse strikes a curiously familiar chord in the current American political environment of absolutes. So that when he says at the end of "Why Is We Americans?" "... but we is also to the/end of your silence and sit down,/we is at the end of being under/your ignorant smell your/intentional hell, either give us/our lives or plan to forfeit your/own" there is something of the language that only the most powerful understand how to employ--it is language not unlike the bold, bullying and exclusionary assertions that American politicians have employed recently in their so-called clear-eyed confrontation of what they have defined as the evil of this world. The poem itself is an amazing explosion of the issues that Baraka is contending with as an American here at the cusp of the new century. The lines emerge with the cadence and punch of the Black preacher's jazz improvisation of sound, idea and soul. After retracting his attacks on Martin Luther King, Jr. ("and i know when i was/young i used to run him in the/ground") he embarks on a two-page romp about reparations:

> ... we wants
> the mule the land, you can
> make it threehundred years of
> blue chip stock in the entire
> operation. We want to be paid,
> in a central bank The average
> worker farmer wage for all
> those years we gave it free.
> Plus we want damages, for all
> the killings.the fraud, the
> lynchings, the missing justice,
> the lies and frameups,
> unwarranted jailings, tar and
> featherings, character and
> race assassinations. historical
> slander, ugly caricatures, for
> each sambo, step and fechit
> damon wayans flick,
> we want to be paid, for
> every hurtful thing you did or
> said. for all the land you took,
> for all the rapes, all the
> rosewoods ...

He goes on to call for reparations for all who have been consumed and exploited by a system that begins to read as a capitalistic monstrosity:

> ... for the
> native peoples even the poor
> white people you show all the
> time as funny, all them abners
> and daisy maes, them beverly
> hill billies who never got to no
> beverly hills. who never got to
> harvard on they grandfather's
> wills. we want reparations for
> them, right on, for the
> mexicans whose land you
> stole. ...

It ought to be clear to any reader who reads as far as this poem in the book that Baraka's politics are clear even if troubling to some. The curiosity about the title poem, "Somebody Blew Up America," is that it amounts to one grand question that should be rhetorical. The poem is a catalogue poem--a poem that lists all the atrocities that have been perpetuated by what should be clear to us, is Baraka's enemy. He does not shirk away from the idea that the atrocities have been perpetuated by a conspiracy of ideologies and political motivations. For Baraka, then, the enemy is not hard to identify. The enemy, in this sense, is not unlike the entity called Babylon by the RasTafarians. In many of his later songs, Bob Marley would present similar catalogues of the atrocities carried out by what he called the "Babylon System":

> The Babylon System is a vampire
> Sucking the blood of the sufferer
> Building church and university
> Deceiving the people continually
> Graduating thieves and murderers
> They sucking the blood of the sufferah.

Marley, though, along with many reggae artists, seemed more willing to recognize the complicity of his people and himself in the corruption of Babylon. Marley was at least troubled by the fact that he lived in Babylon instead of in the Promised

Land of Ethiopia. But then, Marley's was a religious belief--
one predicated on the idea that he is merely a sojourner in
this world of Babylon. Baraka's faith is in political systems,
and he openly admits that home for him is the USA. So, in
this poem of protest, he employs the collectivist principles of
Babylon as a system and force to lay out exactly what he re-
gards as the abuses of Babylon. For him the motivation for
the Beast is greed and power. He rarely, if ever, speaks of evil.
His is a secularist conception.

So he presents his case through a catalogue of atrocities,
the device of the rhetorical question. It is clear, however,
from the reaction the poem has received, that the question is
not as rhetorical as Baraka would have imagined. What is
clearer, actually, is that rhetorical questions are dependent
on shared notions of social and political history. Some peo-
ple would respond to the question, "Would a father betray
his son?" with the answer "yes." Anyone who works his or
her way through Baraka's poem will realize one simple truth,
his answer to his question of "who blew up America" is not,
as some have suggested, the Jewish people, but, in fact, *pax*
anglo-Saxon America--wealthy, conservative America and the
very historical philosophies that undergird such a communi-
ty. Christians ought to be more offended and disturbed by Ba-
raka's statements than Jews. In the same poem he seems to
make it quite clear:

> Who put the Jews in ovens,
> And who helped them do it
> Who said "America First"
>
>> And ok'd the yellow stars
>
> WHO/WHO/
>
> Who killed Rosa Luxembourg, Liebnecht
> Who murdered the Rosenbergs
> And all the good people iced,

In another telling series of questions, he makes it clear that

Judaism is not the object of his attack:

> Who the Beast in Revelations
> Who 666
> Who decide
> Jesus get crucified

Not who crucified Jesus, but who decided he should be crucified. Thus, in the lines that are the ones that have created the greatest attention and that are said to have led to the effort to remove Baraka as Poet Laureate (2002-2004) of New Jersey because of their anti-Semitic content, we can see that some important processes have to be enacted for it to work in that way. The first is to assume that some of Baraka's less than flatteringcomments about Jews in other and earlier works continue to shape his thinking here. The second is to ignore a distinction that he seems intent on making between Jews and Israelis and the Israeli government. Here there has to be a conflation of the two entities--an act that is understandable if Israel is read as a religious nation state. The history of the formation of the state of Israel makes this a tempting proposition, but it is worth noting that Baraka's poem does not begin with that premise. The third process would be to completely ignore the rhetorical intention of the poem and the central object of the poet's ire. Baraka's quarrel is more clearly with George Bush, Jerry Falwell, and what he views as racist America than with Jews. Perhaps it is this that may have made the move to remove him from the position of Poet Laureate so possible and so likely. Perhaps it is those arbiters of power who recognized that they were quite squarely under attack in Baraka's poem.

The poem itself is a lively and quite sophisticatedly written sound poem that puns cleverly on the hoot of the owl--a questioning wise creature who keeps asking "who?" It is a fluid free fall of energy that combines the tight repetition of "who":

> Who killed the most niggers
> Who killed the most Jews
> Who killed the most Italians
> Who killed the most Irish
> Who killed the most Africans
> Who killed the most Japanese
> Who killed the most Latinos

to the accumulative force of the listing of names;

> Assata, Mumia, Garvey, Dashiell Hammett, Alphaeus
> Hutton, who killed Huey Newton, Fred Hampton
> Medgar Evers, Mikey Smith, Walter Rodney,

One may be better off and on surer ground quarreling with the easy Manichaeism and somewhat uncomplicated look at history when he concludes that the same people killed Medgar Evers (Southern white supremacists); Mikey Smith (Black Jamaican political thugs) and Walter Rodney (allegedly the henchmen of a Black national leader). This kind of conflation works for Baraka because as we have seen in other poems, his aim is not to name the enemy by describing him, but to suggest that the enemy is best defined by what he destroys and who he destroys. When these men were killed, they were killed for their resistance to those who would deprive people of their freedom to speak against the imperialist power of American and European hegemony.

There is much to be said for the idea that in the US today, poetry can still rouse passions and lead to political action. The problem is that today's United States, driven by the sound byte and video clip--the startling, undigested discourse of television and talk-radio--makes it unlikely that poetry will be read in all its nuance and complexity. Much has been written and said about the role of poetry in US society since the terrorist attacks on September 11, 2001. Alice Walker admitted that prior to that moment, she was convinced that she would not write again. Whole journal issues were devoted to poems responding to the tragedy and virtually every journal or writing contest in the USA has been inundated with poems about the incident. For the most part, the expected response has been characterized by lament, regret, and patriotism. A collective requiem for the victims and for the loss of innocence has shaped much of what has been acceptable in that context. Perhaps what has disturbed many about Baraka's response is that he has not taken up that note. Instead, he has tried to question the assumptions that have marked the orthodox response to the tragedy. In that act he has alienated many and angered others, but he has also compelled America to contend with the very freedoms that it seeks to celebrate. It is the USA that says that Baraka has the right to speak his mind. He knows this, and he is unequivocal about this in his poetry:

> We will only talk of voluntary
> unity, of autonomy, as vective
> arms of self-determination. If
> there is democracy in you that
> is where it will be shown. ...
> ("Why Is We Americans?")

Then for those whose knee-jerk response is to say, "Well if you don't like it here go somewhere else..." he responds:

> ... I be here,
> aint gone nowhere, aint got no
> other, ask your self, no close
> as me relation.

Somebody Blew Up America & Other Poems is an American collection. It is a collection that must be read by anyone who wants to understand that within the nation state of the United States of America are multiple voices that are seeking to defy the homogenized vision of a nation with one voice. It also seeks to defy the remarkably effective political simplification of American society that, through the media, identifies someone like Bill Clinton as ultra left wing and anything further left as belonging to the world of an insane fringe.

Baraka is not so much interested in working within the confines set by his society. He wants to shatter these confines. Tellingly, Baraka has been characterized as an absolute radical--a fanatic, a ranting mad leftist. Hardcore left wing people outside of the US will probably find Baraka's poetry quite moderate in its politics, and maybe that is why it is interesting to have his work published outside the USA. His book, therefore, tells us more about America than about Amiri Baraka himself. At the end of the day, one suspects that this is precisely what Baraka hoped would be the case.

Kwame Dawes
Columbia, South Carolina
2003

Angelo Rombley. *Me and the machines.* 2003. Digital illustration. 7.3″ x 10″.

BEGINNINGS: MALCOLM

(*Airconditioned Nightmare*, by Duke Ellington)

When the Beast emerged from the western sea
as a fictitious ghost who was an actual ghost
to the niggers He carried in his pouch of filth
his Moby Dick ship called Jesus to trick Jesse
and the one legged man who was the Beast
caught the big red Satan and threw him in a cage
disguised in a zoot suit, full of rage, he had fell
from the sky, thought he was an angel, looking
for an angle, a big red Satan, a black devil,
the money lenders created, when his father
was exiled headless in Patmos, looking at sky vision
and the horses ran by stinking up the sky
like an African he thought, his brother had sold
the Beast had bought, he had no soul, and they'd
created money, the animal king, the coin, the khan,
the con, hard currency, the cold return, was a ghost
fools screamed, and he did not exist, not as a ghost
was a Beast who was a man, rose to power in the land
and poor Satan thrown from heaven where he was
white
burned bright red as he fell through the night, but
black
as Ptah, little red desert blood, like a Michigan inferno
blown by the wind, he was Sisyphus too, Elegba if you
insist, legs thrown akimbo, looking for Detroit,
the redman
the redman, was a devil, a nigger, a villainous buck,

a spirit
and an injun, Coltrane and night trane,
iron crazy horse underground railroad
of a heartless heart. He said the ghost is not real, and
neither is God
but when the Prophet called his name, and appeared
in the cage
and his rage turned to love and Allah released him,
because the Beast
was afraid. He swore to uphold the holy almighty soul.
Thought God released him, cold eyed and mannish
a cold nigger punk a murderous skunk
sold dope, found the Beast number and played it like a
game, till the Beast really came
until the Lamb called his name, and freed him
no longer the zoot suit Satan nigger
in jail
unleashed him on the Beast, and the Africans who
were not really Africans cried
ju ju,
and the Beast who was a man and the ghost who
never existed sat across the
evil of money and glistened with evil like slobbering
pain. They called and he turned
but he was never the same.

Even then, when he had left that cage of sin
The Lamb sent a nightingale, wearing the red crescent
of Marvin Gaye, mercy mercy me, O Lamb of Allah,
of black sheep,
of woolly feeling, oh nigger with only three pennies

worth of Dis
in the devil's world. An Egyptian, so old,
was set, no sat, and the bird
a beautiful creature of night's eternity, his desire,
like the burning, was love
not suffocating fire. "Who is that handsome young
minister," said the Prophet's
nurse"? The Prophet not the profit, the good not the
gut, bread is not pain,
money is the jewelry of the bowels.

Was Black Betty there, Betty, beautiful, looking into
the Prophet's eyes
following him inside blackness with the tales of her
fire with the fiery tail
with the kiss divine, like the poet's Amina, sitting there
staring at the once Satanic
issue, like joy from a hidden fissure in the earth,
oh woman of the beginning, oh wife
of the Prophet, O, Lover!

BETTY & MALCOLM

(*Blood Count,* by Billy Strayhorn)

Don Pullen Played

> Duh da Duh
> Dah Duh
> Du

> > Dah Duh Duhhhh
> > Duhhh
> > Duhhhhhh

of that Love
 Bound by Human
   feeling
   as fire & light
     & music
       in the world

> Betty & Malcolm

> > Duh Duh

> > Duh Duh

> > Dah Duh Duhhhh

Yet the earth is not still
 habitable
   for Humans

   & Love is turned
     backwards
     to evil

6

The Live Become The Dead
as Lovers in the Nation
        Lovers of the Nation
        Loved by the Nation
        The oppressed Afro-American
        Nation
            The Nation
            of Islam

"Muhammad Speaks"
    Malcolm was it's founder
    Worker for the Nation
        The Afro-American Nation

But fire ringed around them
from the Beast who is a Man
    & Whisperers & Stinkers
        & Ghosts in Black & White

Malcolm cried, "You Devils!"
But the Devil was near him hiding
    And "Betty", Malcolm sd
        "My Black Sweet Betty",
            as he whistled & hummed
                cooking eggs in the kitchen
                    for the future flowed
                    from him into Betty
                        & out into the world.
"Malcolm", sd Betty,
"DuBois & Garvey were exiled!
    The Lamb, himself, was thrown
    into The Beast's jail.

Be careful Lover Man
Even God can be tricked
& The Prophet told lies
Some brothers work for others
Some sisters are likewise twisted.

"Is it Paradise
or Freedom
that we crave?

"Islam or Liberation
The Religion or The Nation?

The Whisperers whispered
The Stinkers stank
The Beast carried death

Betty's Lover was her husband
Betty's warrior was her man!

Yet the Shriek of the Beast,
"I, Death, will waste you. I can already
taste you!"

Betty cried how many days & nights
She denied it, but even divine
Lovers must have fights. "He was
my Lover, He was my man, He
was my angel, Red & Fierce
for God as he was once as Satan.

"A Love He brought me
Hotter & dug deeper inside me
than Hell, brought Heaven inside
So much sweetness in me made

us laugh made us cry

"Be Careful, Malcolm
    There's Evil in our path.
        Check your back Malcolm
            Be cautious, lover man!"

But light is fire and fire
is in the heart. Malcolm
would not lie
& for this he wd die

                    Who killed
                        him
                    Who killed Malcolm?

Betty was alone now
 into her children
  ringed by the Beast's
   Evil

Oh Hajj Malik
 into Africa to claim
        the vision

Expelled by
The Prophet
  Murdered
    for the profit of the Beast

        Omowale gone home
        Come back alone

            And Betty stared past
            the hour into an

endless weeping & pain
She knew, he was doomed
No matter how her heart
Resisted, Each night
The Beast approached
She heard him
Marching with wet Bloody feet
Six Six Six
Six Six Six

& for a Hollow terrible moment
She screamed
"Malcolm!"
& He was gone

[A1]'

Sister Betty
Malcolm's breath and heart beat
I met in Harlem
When she climbed out the
grave and came back in
the world again

And she screamed at the
Kings and Super Kings, accusing them of
Murder
We saw her many times
& counseled, Sister, It was
Not
those who you say,
yet even they admit
they helped write the last

hours of the play!

Negroes now ran out of
garbage cans with
jewelry & luxurious
vileness
to track her
& taunt her
by claiming to love her
& her dead lover gone
So they cd surround her
with the mediocrity
of empty betrayal
disguised as houses and ex-wives
& lawyers & pretty invitations to
the narrow dancing place
They
And they who are the ghost's
footpersons, threatened to steal
Malcolm's Betty away

But her goodness was
her shield and her mind
leaped like new the Phoenix
Bird toward the Sun.

Dr. Betty
now in the crowded solitude
of mourning
sings memory's bitter
song.

Zig zagged by what she needed

Pushed on & on into
"Cheer The Lonely Traveler"
Remember her travail
Dead Malcolm
told us in her through her
opening, Unity is principal
Betty reach out for
every mind

She was our friend, my wife, Amina,
our children and me

& each year we saw her, she
had stretched out another dimension
toward her own
true self consciousness.

But The Beast Had Tracked
Their Children
Tracked them with
toilet breath
of lies

O, Save Quibilah! we cried
Amina and I
sent Farrakhan a
plea. Just as we sd
to Betty

Struggle is constant
But we must
Unite
Follow the Fire
the Light!

Angelo Rombley. *Had a bad day!...fcuk*. 2003. Digital illustration. 8″ x 7.8″.

IN TOWN

Something in the way of things
Something that will quit and wont start
Something you know but cant stand cant know
But get along with. Like Death riding on top of the car
Peering through the windshield for
His cue. Something entirely fictitious
And true, that creeps across your path
Halloing your evil ways, like they were
Yourself passing yourself not smiling

The dead guy you saw me talking to
Is your boss. I tried to put a spell
On him, but his spirit is illiterate   } *you are your*
I know things you know, and nothing   *boss*
You don't know. Except I saw something
In the way of things, something grinning
At me. And I wanted to know, was it funny
Was it so funny, it followed me down the street
Greeting everybody, like the Good Humor Man
And they got the taste of Good Humor, but no Ice
Cream. It was like that. Me talking across people
Into the houses, and not seeing the beings crowding
Around me with ice picks.   *antagonized*
You cd see them, but they looked
Like important negroes on the way to your funeral.
They looked
Like important jigaboos on the way to your auction.
They let
Them chant the numbers and use an ivory pointer

15

To count your teeth. Remember Step in Fechit.
How we laughed
Knowing it was Sunday School images given flesh and
        jiggling
With the Ice pick high over his head, made you laugh
        anyway.

I can see something in the way of ourselves
That's why I say the things I do. You know it
But it's something else to you. Like that job,
This morning, when you got there, it was quiet
And the machines were yearning soft behind you
Yearning for their nigger to come and give up his life
Standing there being dissed and broke and troubled.

God
vs.
Devil

My mistake is I kept saying that was proof God didn't
        exist
And you told me, Naw, it was proof that the Devil Do.
But still, its like I see something, I hear things,
        I saw words
In the white boy's lying rag said you was gonna die
        poor and frustrated
That them dreams walk with you cross town, is gonna
        die from overwork
That the garbage on the street is telling you you aint
        shit and you almost believe it
Broke and mistaken all the time. You know some of
        the words. But they aint
The right ones. Your cable back on, but aint nothing
        on it you can see
But I see something in the way of things. Something
        make us stumble.

Something get us drunk from noise and addicted to
        sadness. I see something
And feel something stalking us. Like a ugly thing
        floating at our back
Calling us names. You see it, and hear it too, but you
        say it gotta right   God vs.
To exist, just like you. And if God made it, but then   Devil
        we got to argue
And the light go'n come down around us. Even though
        we remember
Where the bank is. Remember the negro squinting at
        us through the cage.

You seen what I see too. A smile that ain't a smile but
        teeth flying against our necks
You see something too, but can't call its name.

Aint it too bad, yall said. Aint it too bad.
Such a nice boy. Always kind to his mother. Always
        say good morning to everybody, on his way to
        work. But that last time before he got locked up
        and hurt
Real bad I seen him walking toward his house and he
        wasn't smiling and he didn't
        even say Hello. But I knew he'd seen
        something. Something in the way of things.
And it worked on him, like it do and will. And he kept
        marching faster and faster
Away from us, and never even muttered a word. Then
        the next day, he was gone!

You wanna know what... what I'm talking about.

Sayin, I seen something something
In the way of things. And how the boy's face looked
that day, just before they took
him away. There is in that face, and remember,
now, remember all them other faces
And all the many places you seen him or the sister
with his child wandering up the
street. Remember what you seen in your own mirror,
and didn' for a second
Recognize the face, your own face, straining to get out
from behind the glass.
Open your mouth like you was gonna say something.
Close your eyes and remember
What you saw, and what it made you feel like. Now
don't you see something else,
Something cold and ugly, not invisible but blended
with the shadow criss crossing
The old man squatting by the drug store at the corner
with his head resting uneasily
On his folded arms. And the boy that smiled. And the
girl he went with, and in my
eyes too, a waving craziness splitting them into the jet
stream of a black bird
His ass on fire, or the solemn notness of where we go
to know we gon' be happy.

I seen something and you seen it too. You just cant
call its name.

Devil?

18

Angelo Rombley. *Standing still*. 2003. Digital illustration. 8″ x 7.9″.

UNDERSTANDING READINESS

For Kwame Toure, who was Stokely Carmichael

(*Johnny Come Lately*, by Billy Strayhorn)

How do we know who we are
>   Except in the world, going through it
>   Together.

How do we know where we are
>   Except with each other
>   Facing reality like dogs
>   Straining on a leash.

How do we know who are our friends and
who are our enemies
>   Only by what they do, who they hold on too,
>   who they fight for and support. Who they help,
>   who they feed in the storm, whose side
>   they're on.

[handwritten margin note: judging based on context]

How do we know who can lead?
>   Only by seeing them do it, only by
>   Feeling the realness and hopefulness,
>   their sincerity, and
>   courage, only by touching their love
>   for the actual selves of us, only

>   By their suffering in our name, the jailings,
>   the beatings and torture, only by the way
>   our enemies describe them,
>   only by their wisdom and plans,
>   their affirmations, their pronouncements and
>   positions, what they think and move on.

freedom What direction they give
us to transform our slave conditions.

Can we name those who are our heroes?
Yes, if we are conscious, even when
they are still alive.

Who is it that will take this brother's place?
All of those who understand what his life was,
what he wanted, what he did, and who, in the
end, he looked to as comrades in struggle,
whatever their names or philosophies
or ideologies or uniforms, or preparation.
All who want democracy and freedom.

How do we know we must struggle, how do we know,
is that why we are
here, to listen again, to see again, to feel again,
can we still ask the brother we celebrate,
whom we loved, whom we still desire
to lift us with his transforming fire!

We know if we call his name he will come, but what
do we need him,
now to do, that he has not already done?

We need him with us, because he is part of us now,
part of our
consciousness and feeling and history.

We need him now, because without him we are not
whole, nor will we go
anywhere but backward,
which he would never do.

How do we speak to him, now?
    with our love, our understanding,
    our developed consciousness.

    We speak to him with our acts,
    with our commitment, with facts,
    with our unyielding will and struggle to be free,
    our self-determination, our soul deep Pledge to
    help unite and liberate oppressed people
    everywhere with the same fierceness we fight
    for Pan Africa, Africa, The Afro-American
    Nation. Is that Clear?

    free
    Africa

And what is this Brother's name?
    Organizer, Black Panther, Lowndes County,
    SNCC, Black Power!, Black United Front,
    Pan-Africa, Nkrumahist, Scientific Socialist,
    Ready for The Revolution,
    Undying Love For The People,
    All African Peoples' Revolutionary Party,
    Stokely Carmichael, Kwame Toure, Comrade,
    Warrior, Ideologue, Thinker, Revolutionary,
    Leader Hero, My Man, Brother!
    Our Dear Brother!!

fighting for freedom
w/ brothers

JUNGLE JIM FLUNKS HIS SCREEN TEST

(*Night in Tunisia*, by Dizzy Gillespie)

James, you shd know
How the world
      Makes you ugly. You is, you know, James
Veddy ugly. You-gly, we used to say
Back in the playground, just touching
      The surface of the thing,
Not understanding that there's ugly, there's You-gly
Then various deeper degrees. Like
Dirty ugly, sick ugly, devil ugly, death ugly
Right on till you get to the bottom of the beginning
Of some shit too ugly to be dug, by mere you man.

I never seen that deepest dirtiest past-serial killer ugly
I seen Bush-2 and his charcoal imp-dummy, Kneel
Bent
I seen a Lott, a Bilbo, a thing wrapped in white sheets
carrying
His burning soul, disguised as a baking nigra eyes
melting
Into snot. I seen somethin' so ugly I cancelled it out
my mind
And if I try to remember I get horizontal lines and
blood come out
My fingers.

Ugly is the first letter of where you is.
Satan begin with an S.
Put together they is money. A collection of ignorant
medusas

greed,
materialism

24

Halloween; piano lessons in a human skin mask polka
dot with blood.
Self is above, dead and unconnected, as if floating.

Defying gravity with the magic of bullshit.

You ugly with and in and because is you was the same
You ugly because you know you ugly and say you
ain't
You ugly because you eat everybody and belch } opposites
Hollywood
You ugly because you like it and you wanna be ugly
and you think ugly
Cute. You uglier than anybody except who made you
ugly, look between yr legs
At the flickering light of skyscraper teeth on fire again,
and some peepas say
God did it. Was either him or somebody else colored.

You ugly because that's how you got rich
But you got more ugly than you got money
With all that money you still ugly.
The ugliest other thing in the world think you ugly
And happy because you make them feel better
You uglier than Agnew. When you get yr Ph.D. in ugly
You will be Hitler's last meal. You uglier than
Churchill
And Bush, the father, hideous wife

Ghouls say you ugly behind yr back
Vampire scared a you
When Clarence Pendleton passed gas it painted your
face all over the room

You uglier than the painting Clarence Thomas got in
the attic
Of his real self which Oscar Wilde did of him
You uglier than Papa Doc, Hitler and Mobutu
You uglier than Mussolini Franco
and the Swedish Angel
Is yr twin. You uglier than zombie vomit.
Uglier than zoo dirt. You the ugliest thing in the
human family
And that ID you got sayin' you human is ugly
You ugly as devil doo doo, white supremacy and you
Is identical. You ugly as the brain emptiness of a
cracker lynch mob.
You ugly as Falwell dressed as Cab Calloway. You
uglier than white people.
You uglier than Armstrong Williams. You and Ashcroft
is movie stars
Among the backward dead. All insects look better than
you. At yr best
You is vomit, rats run away from you,
You is uglier than Dahmer's sweet tooth. You
is uglier than the police. War is yr makeup.
Prison yr altar. Assassination yr
Conversation. You think stealing make you better
looking. Lying gives you an orgasm. Only pain make
you smile. But you so ugly
No smile would stay near your face.
You drink people's tears and paint yr face
With their blood. You so ugly when you sleep
your dreams torture people.

26

The Devil complains when you tell people you him.
The Devil say you uglier than him.
That cd be a trick.
But nobody ever seen the two of yall
Together. But the Devil dress better than you.

Your face is a uniform. Clothes wont let you put them on
You cannot fart because gas refuses to stay in yr ass
You went to Denmark for sexual transformation
But the doctors cd not figure out which sex you were.

You claim not to be dead

You claim the reason you look the way you do
Is not yr fault. "Nature made me like this", you say.
Naturally everything denies it

nature denies it

WHY IS WE AMERICANS?

Because
No how we find
 our selfs
 over here
 in Dis
 Because

 tragic history
 relatives
 mother
 father
 farther

But can slavery
 the evil ghost them
self
 taked us tooked us
 crooked us, niggers
all the way back

was black
now they white

was this is was
 why is we is
do we do say
all kinds…Hey! Eye!!!

Does them we is
 them what
ain't not

          we was

          to them

is us older where the
gone was dead   ok
          was dead

          Why is we
American?

          Say, Hey,
Willie
          Mays, Say
Hey, Say what
          But, you
got to
          tell me

You got to
    tell me
    tell me

Why is we
Americans

Whereever we is
is the same black
belt, ain't never been
free, since we was
          Seit!

Where who
          did
          was?

Why it
there

we want?

Why we
  Americans,
    mother
      fucker

You sir,
        tell
        why we
        Americans
        dumb
            bastard

        is you is
            sucker

!!!!!!!

(missing section)

i is was for you that them say.
no burn is nothing.
As if, ok.

but how is we then, by that
americans? by what....
        by burn
American by scar
b/c   ? by slavery
oppression by ghetto and darkness in the
        night of pain

30

for race a dumb idea, to be a
thing that is bet upon
How we be then them. how we
be that" say

why is we, then, they who it is
you say, americans.

was they them Americans
with us in the fields. not as
bush one or two. to say Work
nigger work. was they there,
any. who felt the pain of whip
and still was hip. how is we
americans. we never lived with
they.
we lived as coltrane to
lawrence welk. as if
the corniness was a rat with a
whip. how is we they.
how is we americans, was on
paper. ok. dig that. but then
and when
was the bottom of the boat we
constitution. was the burlap we
was slick in.the pig trough they
feed our kids. the took away
drum. that be it.
was I at I
was it slow we can be that
made us that, like ellic
on the screen, is franco still

American vs.
American

31

dead. Boss, was that we ask
that slick, it brings us in. was
the lynchings did it. the kkk???
was it
malcolm dead or dr king, was
that the thing
that did it, made us like them
americans. as we is supposed
to be

look dumb sunofa bitch, if you
say
you got to tell me what way,
we is, i cant see. i know the
paper words. the 13, 14, 15
shit, and nobody even ask
for that, dirty rat, we wanted
free. the mule, the forty
acres. was cool. but that was
like American, it never got here
to us./ you got a line. tell it. i
aint goin no where
that aim't what am said. i want
to know, paper gone,
what is it, the hoods of them
that lynched us. Guiliani's
shining head. Bilbo
without a icepick in his neck.
or Helms
allowed to walk and not be
dead. what is it. Robeson

torture, or W.E.B.
exile with garvey, nat turner
hung, langston before
the unamerican dung. was the ⎫ made American
stripes on us that matched the ⎭ b/c oppression
flag, did it.
the drums they took. the soul
they got, they crooked. from
we, elvis king, indeed, of
greed. What made it what you
say. if robber rip yr dust you
say it must then
be hisn, then why is we is
prison. what is that, you want
believe, why is i
american.

I say I be here anyway, to take
my self to me. I ain't bleed for
you
alone, I bleed from and to my
me. I ain't not american, at
least not
like you and them. I be here,
aint gone nowhere, aint got no
other, ask your self, no close
as me relation. and to begin, if
talk we is, there got to be
reparation. And with that, and
most of all is, am so,
self-determination.

You want to say with eyes
turned out it mean to separate.
that in it
if I want it, otherwise if out
dont be there, how it be my
mind is what be saying,
however, what it is, is what I
say, what I want and do. aint
nobody got no right, no way to
make me what they do. dr king,
my man, say, no lie can live
forever, he say, my man, dr
king, and i know when i was
young i used to run him in the
ground. he say, anyway, no lie,
you dig, like all that shit you
get high on, it cant last,
noway
can it be, forever. and further
deep, make chumps lose sleep,
dr king say you still reap, jive
ass sucker, its deep, aint it,
but you still
reap what you sow.

What i want is me. for
real. i want me and my self.
and what that is is what i be
and what I see and feel and
who is me in the. what it is, is
who it is, and when it me its

what it be....i'm gon' be here,
if I want, like I said, self-
determination, but I aint come
from a foolish tribe, we wants
the mule the land, you can
make it threehundred years of
blue chip stock in the entire
operation. We want to be paid,
in a central bank The average
worker farmer wage for all
those years we gave it free.

Compensation

Plus we want damages, for all
the killings.the fraud, the
lynchings, the missing justice,
the lies and frameups,
unwarranted jailings, tar and
featherings, character and
race assassinations. historical
slander, ugly caricatures, for
each sambo, step and fechit
damon wayans flick,
we want to be paid, for
every hurtful thing you did or
said. for all the land you took,
for all the rapes, all the
rosewoods and black wall
streets you destroyed. all the
miseducation, jobs loss,
segregated shacks we lived in,
the disease that ate and killed
us, for all the mad police that

35

drilled us. For all the music and
dances you stole. The styles.
the language. the hip clothes
you copped. the careers you
stopped. all these are suits,
specific litigation, as
represent we be like we,for
reparations for damages paid
to the Afro-American nation.

lost
culture

We want education
for all of us and anyone else in
the belt hurt by slavery. for the
native peoples even the poor
white people you show all the
time as funny, all them abners
and daisy maes, them beverly
hill billies who never got to no
beverly hills. who never got to
harvard on they grandfather's
wills. we want reparations for
them, right on, for the
mexicans whose land you
stole. for all of north mexico
you call texas, arizona,
california, new mexico,
colorado, all that you gotta
give up, autonomy and
reparations. to the Chicano,
and the Native Americans, whose
souls you ripped out with their

land, give Self-Determination,
Regional Autonomy, that's what
my we is askin, and they gon
do the same. when they
demand it, like us again, but,
in they own exploited name.
Yeh the education thats right
two hundred years. But we
want all the cash, we want a
central stash, a central bank,
with democratically elected
trustees, and board elected by
us all, to map out, from the
referendum we set up, what we
want to spend it on. To build
that Malcolm sense Self
Determination as Self
Reliance, Self Respect, Self
Defense, the will of what the
good Dr. DuBois beat on "true self
consciousness".Simply the
psychology of Freedom.
        Then we can talk
about bein american. then we
can listen without the...the
undercurrent of desire to first
set your ass on fire.
We will only talk of voluntary
unity, of autonomy, as vective
arms of self-determination. If
there is democracy in you that

heed compensation to achieve peaceful feelings

37

is where it will be shown. this
is the only way we is
americans. this is the only
truth that can be told.
otherwise there is no future
between us but war. and we is
rather lovers and singers and
dancers and poets and
drummers and actors and
runners and elegant
heartbeats of the sun's
flame....but we is also to the
end of our silence and sit down.
we is at the end of being under
your ignorant smell your
intentional hell. either give us
our lives or plan to forfeit your
own.

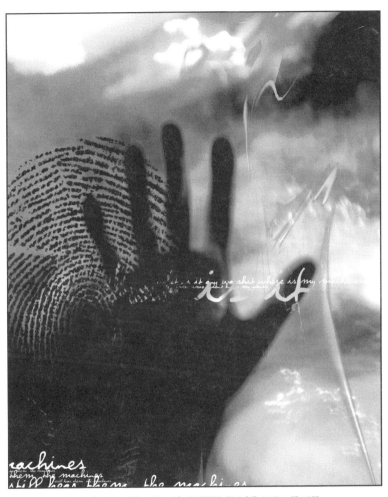

Angelo Rombley. *Where is my identity?* 2003. Digital illustration. 8″ x 10″.

SOMEBODY
BLEW UP
AMERICA

(All thinking people
oppose terrorism
both domestic
& international...
But one should not
be used
to cover the other)

They say its some terrorist, some

    barbaric

        A Rab, in

    Afghanistan

                It wasn't our American terrorists
                It wasn't the Klan or the Skin heads
                Or the them that blows up nigger
                Churches, or reincarnates us on Death row

It wasn't Trent Lott
Or David Duke or Giuliani
Or Schundler, Helms retiring

It wasn't
the gonorrhea in costume
the white sheet diseases
That have murdered black people
Terrorized reason and sanity
Most of humanity, as they pleases

41

They say (who say? Who do the saying)

                              Who is them paying
                                Who tell the lies
                                Who in disguise
                               Who had the slaves
                        Who got the bux out the Bucks

                          Who got fat from plantations
                            Who genocided Indians
                        Tried to waste the Black nation

                              Who live on Wall Street
                                The first plantation
                               Who cut your nuts off
                                Who rape your ma
                                Who lynched your pa

Who got the tar, who got the feathers
Who had the match, who set the fires
Who killed and hired
Who say they God & still be the Devil

                                Who the biggest only
                                Who the most goodest
                               Who do Jesus resemble

                              Who created everything
                                 Who the smartest
                                 Who the greatest
                                 Who the richest

Who say you ugly and they the goodlookingest

Who define art
Who define science
Who made the bombs
Who made the guns
Who bought the slaves, who sold them

Who called you them names

Who say Dahmer wasn't insane

Who/   Who/   Who/

Who stole Puerto Rico
Who stole the Indies, the Philippines, Manhattan
Australia & The Hebrides
Who forced opium on the Chinese

Who own them buildings
Who got the money
Who think you funny
Who locked you up

Who own the papers
Who owned the slave ship
Who run the army

Who the fake president
Who the ruler
Who the banker

Who/   Who/   Who/

Who own the mine
Who twist your mind
Who got bread
Who need peace

Who you think need war

Who own the oil
Who do no toil
Who own the soil
Who is not a nigger
Who is so great ain't nobody bigger

Who own this city

Who own the air
Who own the water
Who own your crib
Who rob and steal and cheat and murder
and make lies the truth

                    Who call you uncouth

Who live in the biggest house
Who do the biggest crime
Who go on vacation anytime

Who killed the most niggers
Who killed the most Jews
Who killed the most Italians

Who killed the most Irish
Who killed the most Africans
Who killed the most Japanese
Who killed the most Latinos

Who/ Who/ Who/

Who own the ocean
Who own the airplanes
Who own the malls
Who own television
Who own radio

Who own what ain't even known to be owned

    Who own the owners that ain't the real owners

                Who own the suburbs
                Who suck the cities
                Who make the laws

Who made Bush president
    Who believe the confederate flag need to be flying
        Who talk about democracy and be lying
            WHO/ WHO/ WHOWHO/
                Who the Beast in Revelations
                    Who 666 *Devil*
                  Who decide
                Jesus get crucified

45

Who the Devil on the real side
Who got rich from Armenian genocide

                              Who the biggest terrorist
                              Who change the Bible
                              Who killed the most people
                              Who do the most evil
                              Who don't worry about survival

Who have the colonies
Who stole the most land
Who rule the world
Who say they good but only do evil
Who the biggest executioner

                    Who/Who/Who

Who own the oil
Who want more oil

Who told you what you think that later you find out a lie

                              Who/ Who/ ???

Who fount Bin Laden, maybe they Satan
Who pay the CIA
Who knew the bomb was gonna blow
Who know why the terrorists
Learned to fly in Florida, San Diego

Who know why Five Israelis was filming the explosion
        And cracking they sides at the notion

46

Who need fossil fuel when the sun ain't goin' nowhere

                    Who make the credit cards
                    Who get the biggest tax cut

        Who walked out of the Conference
        Against Racism

Who killed Malcolm, Kennedy & his Brother
Who killed Dr King, Who would want such a thing?

        Are they linked to the murder of Lincoln?

Who invaded Grenada
Who made money from apartheid
Who keep the Irish a colony
Who overthrow Chile and Nicaragua later

            Who killed David Sibeko, Chris Hani,
            The same ones who killed Biko, Cabral,
            Neruda, Allende, Che Guevara, Sandino

    Who killed Kabila, the ones who wasted Lumumba
        Mondlane, Betty Shabazz, Princess Di, Ralph
                        Featherstone
                        Little Bobby

        Locked up Mandela, Dhoruba, Geronimo,

    Assata, Mumia, Garvey, Dashiell Hammett, Alphaeus
        Hutton, who killed Huey Newton, Fred Hampton
        Medgar Evers, Mikey Smith, Walter Rodney,

Was it the ones who tried to poison Fidel
Who tried to keep the Vietnamese Oppressed
Who put a price on Lenin's head

Who put the Jews in ovens,
And who helped them do it
Who said "America First"

    And ok'd the yellow stars

               WHO/WHO/

Who killed Rosa Luxembourg, Liebnecht
Who murdered the Rosenbergs
And all the good people iced,
Tortured , assassinated, vanished

           Who got rich from Algeria, Libya, Haiti,
              Iran, Iraq, Saudi, Kuwait, Lebanon,
                 Syria, Egypt, Jordan, Palestine,

Who cut off peoples hands in the Congo
Who invented Aids Who put the germs
In the Indians' blankets

Who thought up "The Trail of Tears"
Who blew up the Maine
& started the Spanish American War

Who got Sharon back in Power
Who backed Batista, Hitler, Bilbo,
Chiang Kai-shek

who WHO W H O

Who decided Affirmative Action had to go
Reconstruction, The New Deal,
The New Frontier, The Great Society,

Who do Tom Ass Clarence Work for

Who doo doo come out the Colon's mouth

Who know what kind of Skeeza is a Condoleeza

Who pay Connelly to be a wooden negro

Who give Genius Awards to Homo Locus Subsidere

Who overthrew Nkrumah, Bishop,
Who poison Robeson
Who try to put DuBois in Jail
Who frame Rap Jamil al Amin
Who frame the Rosenbergs, Garvey,
The Scottsboro Boys
The Hollywood Ten

Who set the Reichstag Fire

Who knew the World Trade Center was gonna get
bombed

Who told 4000 Israeli workers at the Twin Towers
to stay home that day

Why did Sharon stay away ?

Who,Who, Who/

explosion of Owl the newspaper say
the devil face cd be seen

Who WHO   Who WHO

Who make money from war

Who make dough from fear and lies
Who want the world like it is

Who want the world to be ruled by imperialism and
national oppression and
terror
violence, and hunger and poverty.

Who is the ruler of Hell?
Who is the most powerful

Who you know ever
                    Seen God?

But everybody seen
                    The Devil

Like an Owl exploding
In your life in your brain in your self
Like an Owl who know the Devil
All night, all day if you listen, Like an Owl
Exploding in fire. We hear the questions rise
In terrible flame like the whistle of a crazy dog

            Like the acid vomit of the fire of Hell
            Who and Who and WHO (+) who who

        Whoooo and whooooooOOOOOOooooOoooo!   Owl

50

POSTSCRIPT: NO BLACK INK IN FAX

SEPT 11, 2001, Reggie woke me with a phone call saying turn on the television. He was driving me to work in Felipe Luciano's election campaign in New York City for city councilman.

When I got the box on, one tower was already half on fire. What a horrible accident went through my mind, as a child who witnessed the hole in the Empire State Building when a plane hit it in the 1940s. But in a minute another air liner turned the corner into that explosion of madness--not just the building but the country and the world--what we now call "9/11"! The number you dial for emergency police presence! But since that craziness, that number signifies the end of "Weimar 2" (the last quasi-democratic government in Germany, before Adolf Hitler!). It was called the Weimar Republic, and once it disappeared into the insanity of German fascism and World War II, it is now summoned to invoke the "Last Days" of humanity in Europe before the concentration camps.

Hitler was legally appointed chancellor by the republic's second president, Paul von Hindenburg, who got in because of a split between the ultra-Left Communists and the fuzzy middle-Social Democrats, some of whom immediately began to attach themselves to the far right.

Bourgeois Democracy ended in terror when the Reichstag, the seat of German political governance, was destroyed by a mysterious fire. Actually, now and for a long time, most people know that Hitler and his fascist fiends set the fire so they could end the "liberal" Weimar era, with a crisis produced by Nazi "Black OPs," which would then permit them to pass the infamous REICHSTAG ENABLEMENT ACT, which allowed the arrest, ersatz trials and subsequent imprisonment of millions of "criminals," beginning with Communists, trade union activists, foreign nationals and ultimately the slaughter of six million Jews in what Hitler characterized as his "Final

51

Solution" to "The Jewish Question"!

In a few ticks Auschwitz opened (1933) followed by similar death traps, complete with gas chambers and crematoria. Interestingly, the first offense listed on Hitler's Racial Laws was inspired by the resurgent US Confederacy's Black Codes, following the Civil War, which plunged Black people back into near slavery!

After I was sunk deep down into my feelings and understanding by the actual terror, when Bush 2 began his shallow call for Americans to rise in fear and patriotism counter-attack against the terrorists, then named Osama Bin Laden, Taliban and al-Qaida, I rejected all of this narcotic. First because Bush, to me, was nothing but an illegal usurper to the US presidency, with actually less legitimacy to lead this country than Hitler had in Germany in 1933!

That was the poem's initial ignition, recalling the objective and outraging fact that Black people have ALWAYS lived in terror in this country from the Slave Trade until this very day!

As I went further and deeper, I began to register the ubiquitous, often mysterious, reign of terror that has been waged against most of the people in the world by a world wide, historic coven of bestial merchant and money hungry merchants, bankers, politicians, capitalists, monopoly capitalists, imperialists, with the continuous interrogative of rhythm demanding WHO(?) were these perpetrators.

On October 1, 2001, just after I finished the poem and reflected on what I had written, I sent the poem across the world on the Internet, and began to read it. It was read in Africa; Portugal, Spain, Switzerland, Italy; on German radio by an actor, and copied internationally. I read it at colleges across the United States, Amherst, Yale, Amherst, University of Chicago, NYU, Iowa, North Carolina, programs of all sorts, venues of various description.

Almost a year later, ApriL 2002, I received a letter saying I had been named NEW JERSEY POET LAUREATE. I received the letter in May, saying the honor would be announced in June, it was finally made public in August by New Jersey Governor McGreevey in a public ceremony to announce the signing of the "Amistad Bill," which makes it mandatory that New Jersey public school textbooks contains the history, culture and lives of the Afro-American people.

As a barbed bit of humor I warned the Governor that day that he was gonna get in trouble for naming me Laureate. He said he could handle it. But after reading the poem at the Dodge Poetry Festival in September before some two thousand or so people, what ensured surprised both of us.

Although I received standing ovations each time I read the poem at the Dodge Festival, and later sat for two hours signing copies of the book, receiving a continuous praise for writing and reading it, three people objected. One, was a man who made a light comment about the lines "Who told 4000 Israeli workers at the Twin Towers/To stay home that day/ Why did Sharon stay away?"

He said he dug the poem but objected to those lines. Then two carefully dressed shadows, who looked like white versions of the bias testers in Gentleman's Agreement approached, arm in arm, inside their Saks Fifth Avenue outfits and said simply, "That was a hateful poem!" and passed.

A few days later, the governor's secretary called me and read a press release from the Anti-Defamation League (ADL), claiming the poem or at least those four lines (out of a three hundred-forty-line poem) were "Anti-Semitic."

The ADL is a notorious Israeli lobbyist, whose fundamental tactic is to call anyone who does not share its fictitious beautification of the state of Israel, "Anti-Semites," then proceed to further slander them. In the press release the ADL asked that I apologize and resign. I told the Governor's secretary and in a few days, the world, I would do neither.

My actual "crime" was that I said that Israel and the US KNEW (so did Germany, France, Russia, England) about the eminent "terrorist" attack on the World Trade Center. And that the Bush criminals did nothing to stop it, but also that Israeli workers in Israeli corporations were warned about the coming terror!

The ADL, *Star Ledger* and other garbage wrapping newspapers, insist that when I say Israeli workers I am saying "Jew" and blaming the terror on Jews.

That, of course, is a lie. But even more dangerous to the ADL and the Zionist lobby and Bush Right warmongers, is that I AM IMPLYING THAT ISRAEL THINKS OF AMERICAN JEWS AS AMERICANS, THAT THEY LET AMERICAN JEWS DIE WITH THE REST OF US, BUT WARNED ISRAELI NA-TIONALS THAT THE MURDERS WERE COMING! (One company's CEO, at ODIGO, has already admitted this publicly. The Israeli embassy's official death toll of Israelis in the WTC madness was FIVE. Two of whom died in the airplanes, out of over 3000 people killed on 9/11.)

At any rate, I have been attacked, slandered, character as-sassinated, lied about! There are ELEVEN BILLS in the New Jersey Legislature calling for my censure, condemnation, re-moval, forfeiture of the $10,000 stipend that goes with the Laureate post! Of course, there are not eleven bills dealing with education, unemployment, racism, housing, or anything else. I have continued to call for a public discussion at a large hall or in the legislature of the poem, asking that it be pro-jected on a screen with the ADL, the Governor and anyone else, pointing out the "Anti-Semitism" in the poem. But they will not even print the rest of the poem.

There is much more tale around this attack on my char-acter and my work, by these "Axholes of Evil" (one should read my initial and following statements to the press at www.

amiribaraka.com).

I will remain the New Jersey Poet Laureate, at least until April 2004, and I will not apologize. I will not resign. As for the poem, who knows the Lord Mayor of London during Shakespeare's time, or the governor or mayor of New York, when similar donkeys made similar charges against Langston Hughes and Paul Robeson and W.E.B. DuBois?

The most important thing about all this is that it is a clear demonstration of the rising stink of fascism in the USA. Minimally, it is an attack on my First Amendment rights.

My parting question should also be considered. The Bush Right's Patriot Bill and Homeland Security are clear evidence of the growth of poisonous anti-democratic forces and institutions in this country. Like the internationally opposed continuum of dishonest, bloodquakes of war that Bush has imposed on the Middle East and the world in just two years (Not to mention absconding from the National Treasury so much money that we have gone from a surplus to a three trillion $ deficit!).

Afghanistan, backing the ethnic cleansing of the Palestinians by the Butcher Sharon, and the completely falsified nazi-like attack on Iraq should make us all, not just in the US, but democratic peoples everywhere, understand that the counterfeit President, Bush 2, is an empty war head of the Far Right, just a few dance steps from fascism! We ask, without 9/11, would any of this be possible. Imagine you are in Germany in 1933, and there in all its terror is THE REICHSTAG FIRE!

- Amiri Baraka 2003 Newark, NJ

ABOUT THE AUTHOR

Amiri Baraka was born in 1934, in Newark, New Jersey, USA. The author of over 40 books of essays, poems, drama, and music history and criticism, Baraka is a poet icon and revolutionary activist who has recited poetry and lectured on cultural and political issues extensively in the USA, the Caribbean, South America, Africa and Europe. The influences on his work range from musical orishas such as Ornette Coleman, John Coltrane, Theophilus Monk and Sun Ra to the Cuban Revolution, Malcolm X and world revolutionary movements. Baraka is renown as the founder of the Black Arts Movement in Harlem in the 1960s, which became, though short-lived, the virtual blueprint for a new American theater aesthetic. The movement and his published and performance work, such as the signature study on African-American music, *Blues People* (1963), and the play, *Dutchman* (1963), practically seeded what has been called the "cultural corollary" to the African-American nationalism of that revolutionary milieu. Other titles range from *Selected Poetry of Amiri Baraka/LeRoi Jones* (1979), to *The Music* (1987), a fascinating collection of poems and monographs on Jazz and Blues authored by Baraka and his wife and poet Amina, and his boldly sortied essays, *The Essence of Reparations* (2003). He has taught at Yale, Columbia and the State University of New York at Stony Brook. *Somebody Blew Up America & Other Poems* is Baraka's first collection of poems published in the Caribbean and includes the title poem that has headlined him in the media in ways rare to poets and authors. The recital of the poem "that mattered" engaged the poet warrior in a battle royal with the very governor of New Jersey and with a legion of detractors demanding his resignation as the state's Poet Laureate because of *Somebody Blew Up America's* provocatively poetic inquiry (in a few lines of the poem) about who knew beforehand about the New York World Trade Center bombings in 2001. The poem's own detonation caused the author's photo and words to be splashed across the pages of New York's *Amsterdam News* and the *New York Times* and to be featured on CNN--to name a few US and international media. Awards and honors include an Obie, the American Academy of Arts & Letters award, the James Weldon Johnson Medal, Rockefeller Foundation and National Endowment for the Arts grants, Professor Emeritus at the State University of New York at Stony Brook, and Poet Laureate of New Jersey.

CORAZÓN DE PELÍCANO
Antología poética de Lasana M. Sekou

PELICAN HEART
An Anthology of Poems by Lasana M. Sekou

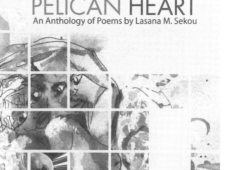

Selección, introducción y notas
Selection with Introduction and Notes by

EMILIO JORGE
RODRÍGUEZ

LASANA M. SEKOU

NATIVITY
NATIVITÉ • NATIVIDAD
t r i l i n g u a l   e d i t i o n

Nativity cover art: Adán, sculpture/bronze and Eva, sculpture/bronze by Fernando Botero. © Fernando Botero. Courtesy: Museo de Antioquia, Colombia.